DEFEATED ENEMIES

from Brad
Christmas 2002

Other Books by Corrie ten Boom

Amazing Love
Common Sense Not Needed
The Hiding Place
Marching Orders for the End Battle
Not Good If Detached
Plenty for Everyone
A Prisoner and Yet...
Tramp for the Lord

DEFEATED ENEMIES

by Corrie ten Boom

CHRISTIAN LITERATURE CRUSADE
Fort Washington, Pennsylvania 19034

CHRISTIAN LITERATURE CRUSADE
Fort Washington, Pennsylvania 19034

CANADA
1440 Mackay Street, Montreal, Quebec

First American Edition 1963
Revised Edition 1970
Fifteenth printing 1975

SBN 87508-021-9

DEFEATED ENEMIES

The Conflict

HAVING faced fights not "against people made of flesh and blood, but against persons without bodies—the evil rulers of the unseen world" (Eph. 6:12 Living NT), in prisons during the war, and later when traveling over the world; and having met so many people—even dear servants of the Lord—who, though surrounded by the powers of darkness, the devil and the demons, do not recognize them, and do not know how to deal with them, I decided, at the request of a missionary friend, to write down what I have learned, as a help for other children of God.

Someone asked my opinion of the missionaries in a certain country. My answer was, "They have given all, but they have not taken all. They have given homeland, time, money, luxury, and more, but they have not taken all the riches abundant that the Word gives us from the boundless resources of God's promises. Many do not know about two precious weapons: the power of the cross and blood of Jesus and every Christian's legal right of the use of the wonderful Name of Jesus."

Mrs. Penn-Lewis wrote, " . . . when the existence of evil spirits is recognized by the heathen, it is generally looked upon by the missionary as 'superstition' and ignorance; whereas the ignorance is often on the part of the missionary, who is blinded by the prince of the power of the air to the revelation given in the Scriptures, concerning the satanic powers."[1]

We need to recognize the enemy, in order to overcome him. But let us beware of the mistakes that C. S. Lewis describes in *The Screwtape Letters*. He says: "There are two equal and opposite errors into which our race can fall about the devils. One is to disbelieve in their existence, the other is to believe and to feel an unhealthy interest in them! They

---

[1] Jessie Penn-Lewis, *War on the Saints* (Christian Literature Crusade), p. 21.

themselves are equally pleased by both errors, and they hail a materialist or a magician with the same delight." [2]

We have a good safeguard and guide, the Bible, God's Word. Here we find not only the necessary information about Satan and demons, but also the weapons and the armor that we need for this battle, so that, through Jesus Christ, we may be more than conquerors.

Let us keep in mind that God wants and expects us to be conquerors over the powers of darkness—not only for the sake of personal victory, and for the liberation of other souls from the chains of Satan (though this is very important—see Isa. 49:24, 25), but for His glory, so that His triumph and victory over His enemies may be demonstrated! Read Col. 2:15; Eph. 3:10; Eph. 1:20-23; 1John 3:8.

First, then, let us see what the Bible says about the powers of darkness. The devil or Satan is introduced to us as a person who opposes God and His work. (See Gen. 3:1; Rom. 15:22.) He is the "god of this world," who blinds the minds of the people to the truths of God's Word (2 Cor. 4:4; Eph. 2:2). Having rebelled against God, he was cast out of heaven; then he caused man's fall in paradise. Jesus calls him the father of lies, a liar, a murderer (John 8:44). He works often as an "angel of light" (2 Cor. 11:14), seeking the ruin of the elect! (1 Peter 5:8). But he was cursed of God. Jesus triumphed over him at the Cross of Calvary (1 John 3:8) and in His resurrection, and he will finally be condemned and destroyed (Rev. 20). There are many kinds of demons, and they afflict people in various ways (see Matt. 12:22, 17:15-18; Luke 13:16). Also, they bring false doctrine (1 Tim. 4:1-4), trying to seduce the elect (Matt. 24:24), oppressing (Acts 10:38), obsessing, and possessing people. They know Jesus, and recognize His power and tremble (Matt. 8:29). For them, hell is the final destination, as it is for Satan.

Secondly, let us consider some references of the Bible concerning the stand we have to take against these powers! It is most important to realize that ours is the position *in*

[2] C. S. Lewis, *The Screwtape Letters* (New York, The Macmillan Co., 1969), p. 3.

Christ, "far above all principality, and power, and might, and dominion . . . " (Eph. 1:21). We are called to resist the devil (James 4:7), in the whole armor of God (Eph. 6:13-18), by virtue of the blood of Jesus (Rev. 12:11), by faith, prayer, and fasting (Matt. 17:20,21). Jesus cast out demons (Matt. 12), and He commands and expects His disciples to do the same. (Read Luke 9 and 10, also Matt. 28:20 and Mark 16-17.) In Acts, we learn how the disciples exercised their authority by casting out demons, thus magnifying the Name of Jesus! (See Acts 8:7.)

Let us remember that God's Word stands forever and that His commandments mean for us today exactly the same as for the disciples 2,000 years ago! Those who act on them, in obedience, will in the same way prove God's almighty power. Yes . . . Jesus said, *"In my name* shall they cast out devils!" (Mark 16:17).

> Last of all I want to remind you that your strength must come from the Lord's mighty power within you. Put on all of God's armor so that you will be able to stand safe against all strategies and tricks of Satan. For we are not fighting against people made of flesh and blood, but against persons without bodies—the evil rulers of the unseen world, those mighty satanic beings and great evil princes of darkness who rule this world; and against huge numbers of wicked spirits in the spirit world. So use every piece of God's armor to resist the enemy whenever he attacks, and when it is all over, you will still be standing up. But to do this, you will need the strong belt of truth and the breastplate of God's approval. Wear shoes that are able to speed you on as you preach the Good News of peace with God. In every battle you will need faith as your shield to stop the fiery arrows aimed at you by Satan. And you will need the helmet of salvation and the sword of the Spirit—which is the Word of God. Pray all the time. Ask God for anything in line with the Holy Spirit's wishes. Plead with Him, reminding Him of your needs, and keep praying earnestly for all Christians everywhere. (Eph. 6:10-18, Living NT).

Have you heard the name of Pastor Blumhardt? Eighty years ago, in Germany, in a place called Möttlingen, he had to face a grim fight with the powers of darkness. One of his faithful parishioners, Gottliebin Dittus became demon possessed, and a battle started which ended victoriously eighteen months later when the last demon went out of the girl. With a loud voice, heard over the whole town, he shouted, "Jesus is victor!" After this, God gave great blessings in Möttlingen. The little town became a center where many Christians received special gifts of healing, and of casting out demons (see 1 Cor. 12:28)!

On his death bed, Pastor Blumhardt prophesied, "Fifty years from now God will give to Möttlingen a man more gifted than I, and greater things will happen than in my time." This is what happended when Father Stanger started his work and opened "Die Arche," a home, where many people found spiritual help, many sick were healed, and many were set free from demon influence. Both my sisters went yearly to that place and told me much about what they learned. Thus I was not altogether unprepared when I came myself into contact with the powers of darkness.

Now, let me tell you about my own experiences, and how I have proved the wonderful power of the blood of Jesus, and of the name of Jesus, and the trustworthiness of His promises! I have already written down some facts in my books, *A Prisoner and Yet, Amazing Love, Not Good if Detached,* and so I will add passages from these books that refer to our subject!

The Sin of Fortunetelling

"There shall not be found among you any one that maketh his son or his daughter pass through the fire, or that useth divination, or an observer of times, or an enchanter, or a witch, or a charmer, or a consulter with familiar spirits, or a wizard, or a necromancer. For all that do these things are an abomination unto the Lord: and because of these abominations the Lord thy God doth drive them out from before thee. Thou shalt be perfect with the Lord thy God" (Deut. 18:10-13).

After the war in Germany there was among many people great uncertainty about the soldiers that were missing. Were they still in Russian concentration camps, or had they died during the fighting? This uncertainty caused great suffering among their relatives, and many people went to fortune-tellers, to find out about their loved ones. I don't know whether they got any real information, but this I know, many came to me and told me about permanent darkness in their hearts and an urge to commit suicide. This symptom is always a sure evidence of demon influence!

A child of God need not remain in darkness, Jesus said. "I am the light of the world: he that followeth me shall not walk in darkness, but shall have the light of life" (John 8:12).

After I had frequently had such confidences, I decided to speak against the sins of occultism, and so in every series of meetings I spoke once on this subject. I used to read Deut. 18:10-13, showing how these sins are an abomination in the sight of God, because they show how one, instead of depending on His power, asked help from the enemy. Then I showed the help that the Bible gives. It is wonderful that the Bible provides an answer to this serious problem! Jesus came to undo the works of Satan. "God openly displayed to the whole world Christ's triumph at the cross where your sins were all taken away" (Col. 2:15b, Living NT).

In the same way that in 2 Kings 6:5, 6 the "son of the prophets" was sent back by Elisha to the place where he had lost the axe and the miracle happened, so I tell people to go back to the place where by their sins they have opened their hearts to the influence of demons, and ask the Lord Jesus to close the door where they have opened it. First, it is necessary to persuade people that they have sinned! Deut. 18:10-13 shows that very clearly. Confession is necessary, and then we may claim the precious promises (1 John 1:7-9) for cleansing. How many I saw liberated instantly when they acted in obedience to this word!

Battle Against the Powers of Darkness

It is wonderful to have an answer to this problem. Jesus came to undo the works of Satan. The Bible says, "They overcame him (Satan) by the blood of the Lamb, and by the word of their testimony . . . " (Rev. 12:11). Ours is the victory through the blood of the Lamb and the testimony of our witness.

Those that are with us are greater than those that are against us. We need not remain in the dark. Jesus said, "I am the light of the world: he that followeth me shall not walk in darkness, but shall have the light of life" (John 8:12). We possess the authority of His name.

What a joy it was to bring the good news of Jesus' victory into the darkness! But whenever I gave this message, I was so tired I could hardly reach my bed. My heart beat irregularly, and I felt ill.

One evening I had a long talk with my heavenly Father. "I cannot continue like this, dear Lord. Why must I give this message, why must I testify against this particular sin? So many of your faithful servants never mention it! I can't go on like this much longer, and live! Perhaps another month or two, and then my heart will give out!"

Then in the Losungsbuch, a daily devotional book in German, I read, "Be not afraid, but speak, and hold not thy peace: For I am with thee, and no man shall set on thee to hurt thee . . . " (Acts 18:9, 10). A short poem follows:

> *Though all the powers of hell attack,*
> *Fear not, Jesus is Victor!*

Joy filled my heart. This was God's answer! I prayed, "Lord, I will obey, I will not fear and be silent. But with my hands on this promise I ask you to protect me with your blood, that the demons cannot touch me."

At that moment something happened to my heart; it beat regularly. I knew that I was healed. After this, when having spoken against sorcery and witchcraft, I felt as well as ever before. Jesus is victor! The fear of demons comes from the demons themselves. We have nothing to fear! He who is with us is greater than those who are against us! Hidden with Christ in God; what a refuge! The mighty High Priest, and His legions of angels, are on our side!

Challenge

In my book *Amazing Love* I tell about May, an intelligent girl in England, who told me that she longed for peace in her heart, but always when she would make a decision to accept Jesus, there was something that kept her back from this step! I said to her, "Listen, May. Think back over the events of your life, and tell me if you have ever been to a fortuneteller. Do you know that when you do such a thing you fall under the curse of it, so that the way to God becomes blocked for you? Yes, even the way to conversion! Such a spell may ensnare you even if you have just allowed yourself to be treated by a mesmerist. Very often such people are also on the wrong side and that may be a great danger."

May laughed in a mocking way. "As a matter of fact, I did allow myself to be persuaded to go to a fortuneteller years ago," she said. "But I did not believe in it, I did it only for fun. Afterwards, we had a real good laugh about it. I had completely forgotten about it, but now, as you ask me, I remember it very well. But surely, there's no harm done, I did not believe it a bit."

"May, suppose you were a soldier during war, and you had to reconnoiter certain terrain. By mistake you fell into the enemy's hands by entering his territory. Do you think that it would help if you then said, 'O excuse me, please, it was not my intention to come here, I just came by mistake'? Once you are on their terrain, you are at their mercy. Though you did not know it, a demon has taken possession of your heart, and your life has fallen under his spell. When you want to be converted, he comes in between. You don't understand the significance of it, and that's why it is so dangerous. Paul says in Eph. 6:12: 'For we wrestle not against flesh and blood, but against principalities, against powers . . . .' "

The look of amusement had left May's face, and fear was there instead.

"I'm not telling you these things to make you afraid, May. If I had no more to say than this, it would have been better to keep silent, but the first step towards victory is to know the enemy's position. And the wonderful thing about it is that Jesus is victor. *He* is far stronger than all the powers of hell. What you have to do is to close the door exactly where you opened it. I mean this; think of some Scripture passages which speak of forgiveness."

May thought for a moment, and then said, "In whom we have redemption through his blood, even the forgiveness of sins" (Col. 1:14).

"That is right. Now ask the Lord Jesus to go back with you to that very moment when you committed that sin. Confess your sin, ask forgiveness, and give thanks for it, because the text which you quoted is true. Then the door is closed, and you are free. Then you are no longer at the demon's mercy.

"I myself once had the opportunity of showing the way of salvation to a fortuneteller. It was in Germany. The whole day long she was busy 'closing doors.' Then she came back to me and said, 'I feel happier, but I know that there are sins which I have forgotten. I am not completely free yet.'

" 'Just tell the Lord Jesus about it as you did me, and give thanks for forgiveness,' I replied.

"Two days later she returned and said, 'This morning I awoke singing. I am completely free.' She was full of praise and thanksgiving to the Lord.

"Will you do it too, May? I know for a certainty that you will be victorious. I'll leave you to yourself now. Fight it out the rest of the way without me."

I left her alone and walked back to the conference grounds. The surf was pounding against the cliffs. A storm was coming up, and it was a tremendous sight. Near the shore a steep rock rose abruptly out of the sea. It was as if two powers fought against each other, but the rock stood unmoved amidst the waves.

On the last night of the conference the leader asked if any would tell what they had learned and experienced these weeks. May stood up and she said, "I have learned and experienced here that Jesus is victor."

A sick woman was sitting in a dirty, messy little kitchen. There was hardly room for my stool. I was eager for a quiet talk with her because she had twice called on a fortuneteller who claimed magic healing power. I told her what a great sin this is in God's sight, because it really means that we run away from God and ask the devil for help. That is why God calls this sin an abomination (Deut. 18:10-12).

A great compassion came into my heart for this woman. I told her about the longing father-heart of God Who loves us so much, and Who brought us into contact with an ocean of love through Jesus Christ. That is why God thinks it so terrible when we seek help from the enemy.

I noticed that she was now listening attentively. When I warned her earnestly, she defended herself and resisted. Now as I told her with joy about that great love of God, she listened intently. I read to her what Jesus said, "Come unto me, all ye that labour and are heavy laden, and I will give you rest" (Matt. 11:28). Before I left, she prayed and asked forgiveness for going to the fortuneteller, and then she praised and thanked God for the great riches she has in Jesus Christ.

Resist the Devil. Ours is the Victory.

In a small town in Germany a group of students planned a weekend. Ten Christians each brought an outsider. Though being the speaker, I felt we were a team, these ten and I! There was much prayer and discussion between the meetings, and when Sunday evening came, eight students had accepted Jesus as their personal Saviour!

Trudy, a medical student, followed me that evening as I, tired but grateful, went to my room. "Corrie, thank you so much for all you have done for Heinz. He is my fiancé. He is so different today! Before, he was all gloom; now he is truly happy!"

"What a joy, Trudy! Let us thank the Lord, for He has done it. I am only a branch of the vine, a channel for His blessing. But tell me, Trudy, what about yourself?"

"I haven't come to speak about myself. I wish only to speak about Heinz."

"Just as you like, then we will speak of the great change in Heinz, who has come out of darkness into God's marvelous light."

Suddenly I turned to Trudy and addressed the demons in her. In Jesus' name I bade them leave and go back to hell, where they belong. I saw immediately a great change in Trudy's face. Astounded, she asked, "Is there hope for me?" Then she fell on her knees and cried, "I am free, thank you, Lord, I am free."

With deep joy Trudy praised the Lord, then confessed she had contemplated committing suicide the next day. Looking into her eyes, I could see she was not entirely free, but she left my room praising the Lord. My legs were trembling. I had known nothing about the girl, and all this seemed to have happened outside of myself. What a victory! Though it was late, I went downstairs to find someone to join me in prayer. In the meeting room I found all the students on their knees.

"I've come to tell you that Trudy is free."

"Yes, we know!"

"What do you know? Who told you?"

"We knew she was under the influence of demons. When we saw her go to your room we all knelt in prayer and asked God to use you to deliver her. Suddenly our prayer became praise, and we knew she was free."

"She is not entirely free. Keep on praying for her until she is completely liberated."

Three days later I spoke at the University which Trudy attends, but she hid behind others. The boys asked me to speak to her, but I had no guidance. A week later, she looked me up in a town where I was working, and God used me to finish the work He had begun in her.

I am well aware I do not possess any special gift for casting out demons, but in times of emergency we must dare to lay hold on the promise of Mark 16:17, "In my name shall they cast out devils."

More Than Psychology

Psychology is profitable, even necessary, but not enough. I recall a conversation with a German pastor. It had been a busy and difficult counseling session. Six people had complained about great inner darkness and thoughts of suicide. Some I had been able to help, but not all.

"Can't you help me?" I asked the pastor. "In cases like these, working together is so much better! One can pray, while the other casts out demons."

The pastor answered me with a discourse on the defense mechanism of the subconscious. That was no help to me! How dangerous to try to solve great problems with small answers.

A theological professor was asked, "Do you teach your students to cast out demons?"

"Hardly," was the answer. "I can't do that myself."

"But you dare to send your students to congregations that are filled with sorcery? Do you think their knowledge of the Jahwist and the Elohist manuscripts of Genesis will help them when they are struggling with the demons that have entered so many people of our day?"

> Soldiers of Christ, arise,
> And put your armour on,
> Strong in the strength which God supplies
> Through His eternal Son.
> Strong in the Lord of hosts
> And in His mighty power.
> Who in the strength of Jesus trusts
> Is more than conqueror.
>
> Leave no unguarded place,
> No weakness of the soul,
> Take every virtue, every grace
> And fortify the whole.
> From strength to strength go on,
> Wrestle and fight and pray,
> Tread all the powers of darkness down
> And win the well-fought day.
>
> *Charles Wesley.*

There are mental diseases to which men are subject but you can find them described in other books. I will confine myself to speaking of the influence that demons exercise on human beings. E. Flöring, a medical doctor, writes about what she learned:

We can distinguish between demon possession and demon obsession. The distinction refers more or less to the intensity with which demoniac forces have invaded or befallen a person, and with which they stick to that person, or whether they come and go, staying only for certain periods, in between which the person seems to be free and quite normal. According to the number and stickability of the demons, the symptoms of the befallen person will vary from occasional abnormal behavior and subjective abnormal sensations (such as strange voices and thoughts—for example, the urge for murder or suicide, or ever recurring fear of various forms and different types) to more abiding, constant expressions of demoniac character: such as abhorring the name of Jesus, and cursing, and negative reaction when the blood of Jesus is mentioned, and strong dislike of the Bible, expressions of hatred when confronted with the gospel, seemingly unchangeable hardness of heart towards the appeal for repentance, in spite of others' prayers—together with physical symptoms, such as grotesque movements (even dances), strange voices speaking through the person, often with a sound that differs from the person's normal voice, sometimes shrieking; or paralysis of one or more parts of the body, or convulsions and cramps of various kinds, the person sometimes being thrown on the ground. Allergic signs are often present, such as skin alterations, or asthma of various grades of severity. Also, there may be a strange expression of the eyes which looks wild or fearful. Heart sensations of varying character, as well as a strong smell, are often found—either one or the other of these symptoms, or more of them combined.

In the prehistory of the person, there has mostly been some connection, either personally or through a member of the family, with witchcraft, or sorcery, or magic (black and white), or fortunetelling, wearing of charms or amulets, or contact with false doctrines, or with persons who exercise demoniac influence, such as witchdoctors and medicine men and fortunetellers, or "wise women", or spiritists and radiesthesists, or people who foretell the future from cards or from the lines of one's hand. All these are spiritual influences that make a person's heart receptive to the powers of evil.

Careless dealing with the sin of others, and with demon-befallen persons, can lead to being attacked by demons! Not in vain does Paul exhort Timothy to keep himself diligently.

In practice it may often not be possible to discern between a demon obsession and a demon possession, as the border line cannot be strictly drawn. This does not matter, as far as the method of help is concerned, because the approach to the demon-befallen person will be the same: in the name of Jesus, in the power of His precious blood, by faith and prayer, and, if necessary, fasting, casting out the demons. However, the intensity of the fight will be harder, the enemy more resistant in the case of a possessed person, the battle may last a longer time, until victory is won.

In my own experience, I have heard a demon-possessed human being speaking with a voice different from his own. It can be that a woman speaks with a male voice the moment she is possessed. The expression of the eyes can be terrible! Often demons spread a smell around them! In Berlin, I had to throw open all the windows when a mother who had accepted the Lord as her Saviour the day before, brought her demon-possessed daughter to me. After the demons had left the girl, the atmosphere was absolutely clear, the smell had disappeared, along with the demons.

The words "demon possessed" must not be used more frequently than it is actually true! When, for example, someone has to suffer from a difficult mother-in-law, she is often too quickly, and perhaps quite unjustly, described as demon-possessed.

Both demon obsession and demon possession are often the result of occult sin, even those from years ago, and now nearly forgotten, and even entered into "just for fun." This includes contact with hypnotism and all the disobedience spoken of in Deut:18:10-13. Remember that Gottliebin Dittus was a girl from a Christian home, but had dealt with magic! (See page 8.) And she became possessed by many demons. Her liberation took one and a half years of faithful wrestling and praying by Blumhardt, assisted by many praying Christians. In Matt. 17:21 the Lord Jesus speaks about a kind of demon that "goeth not out but by prayer and fasting."

In Ravensbrück, the prison camp where my sister Betsie and I were in 1944, we had very little to eat. Betsie once said, "Let us dedicate this involuntary fasting to the Lord, that it may become a blessing." After that, we had experiences of victory over the demons around us.

I am so glad that God does not ask us to give a clear diagnosis. We may simply act on His Word, and we experience that God "watches over His Word to perform it" (Jer. 1:12). What a joy to see an immediate victory through Jesus Christ's power as with the girl in Berlin! Sometimes, the Lord performs the miracle later. In Switzerland, a time of waiting was clearly in God's plan, for it worked out for the opening of the eyes of a minister.

In my book *Amazing Love,* page 75, I write:

Callers arrived to see me; a mother and her fifteen-year-old daughter. The child was a pitiful sight, for she cringed in fear at the slightest sound and buried her face in her mother's arm. The mother's face was full of sorrow as she looked at me pleadingly.

"You spoke last night on the reality of the promises of God," she said. "Do you believe that, yourself?"

"Yes, I do," I answered instantly. "God's promises are a greater reality than our problems."

"Then for Christ's sake, cast out this demon," she said vehemently.

I shrank back as though she had struck me. Anything, but not that! That was a terrain on which I did not want to venture. Other people might be able to do so, but not I.

I prayed silently and asked, "Lord, you know that I cannot and will not do this."

The Lord answered me clearly and unmistakably. "But you must do it, because there is even more truth in what you just said to the woman than you yourself realize. My promises are true."

The mother and I read Mark 16, and then we prayed together and asked Jesus Christ to cover us with His blood, and give safe protection in every struggle against, or attack of the devil.

I asked the child, "Do you know the Lord Jesus?"

"Yes," she said, "but I wish He would make me happy. I want to be happy."

Then I spoke to the demon in the name of the Lord Jesus, who has gained the victory on the cross and has cleansed us with His blood. In His name I commanded the demon to come out of the girl and to go back to hell, where he belonged. I forbade him to enter anyone else or to possess the child again.

The poor girl left the manse as much possessed as when she came, and I was profoundly unhappy. How weak I was in faith, and how lacking in power! Was it only theory that I had been preaching, theory that failed when I tried to put it into practice?

I knocked on the door of the minister's study. He received me kindly. "I need your help," I said. "My faith was too small, and now you will have to do it," and I told him about my experience.

He looked up at me, startled, and said, "Oh, that is a sphere I refuse to enter."

"But who must do it then? You are the shepherd of this flock, and you have God's promises. Please read St. Mark 16:17."

He took his Bible and read, "And these signs shall follow them that believe; in my name shall they cast out devils . . . " And verse 20: "And they went forth, and preached everywhere, the Lord working with them, and confirming the word with signs following."

The minister buried his face in his hands. His reading changed to prayer, and I heard him whisper, "Forgive me, Lord, for I have neglected my duty."

Great joy entered my heart. This was the reason I had to experience the failure of my own attempt. This shepherd had to learn something, and God used me as His instrument.

When I left in the evening there was no darkness, but only gratitude in my heart. There was still much that I didn't understand, but everything was all right.

Jesus is Victor.

Two days later I received a letter from the manse.

"Corrie, something wonderful has happened. When the mother and her daughter crossed the threshold of their home the demon went out of the child. This morning both of them came to me full of praise and thanksgiving to Him who was so faithful about the promises He made to us in the Scripture. My husband wants to know if you will come again, and this time stay longer than three days."

But I knew that this would not be necessary. Jesus is Victor, and He uses everyone who is willing to obey Him.

> *"Whate'er the love of God would do*
> *Is never by His power denied."*

Several times I experienced seeming defeat. They are the darkest moments of my life. I am not called to stay long in one place, and so I must often stop my efforts too early. I always hand the cases over to faithful Christians, if they are available. What I always do in such moments is, that I pray God may search my heart and show me if somewhere is an unconfessed sin (Ps. 139:23, 24). If we are disobedient in anything, we ally ourselves with the enemy! This prayer for heart searching, and—after God has shown us sin—immediately confessing and claiming forgiveness on the ground of 1 John 1:7-9, is necessary in every battle with the enemy where he demonstrates his power in demon-possessed and demon-obsessed people. We are on dangerous ground, and anything of trust in ourselves, love of money, pride, fear, resentment, or any other sin that blocks the channel, makes us powerless and must therefore instantly be brought under the cleansing blood of Jesus. This is also absolutely necessary for Christians who assist. Whenever it is possible, I like to be together with another child of God. One can be in prayer during the whole process, while the other deals with the sinner.

The Sword of the Spirit—God's Word

As I said before there is much witchcraft in Germany. One of the forms with which I came in contact was "the letter from Heaven." This contains strange words and sentences, preceded by an introduction that says that the letter comes straight from the Lord Jesus Himself. It promises good luck and protection from danger.

In Berlin I saw an old man in the audience who hungrily listened to my talk. After the meeting I spoke to him and asked, "Did you ever receive Jesus as your Saviour?" "No," was the answer. "I am sure you want to do it," I said. "I read in your eyes a longing for peace of heart! Jesus can and will give you that, when you ask *Him* to come in. He has knocked at the door, you have heard His voice, and He will come in, when you open your heart. Rev. 3:20 says, 'Behold, I stand at the door and knock: if any man hear my voice, and open the door, I will come in to him . . . .'"

"It is not necessary for me," he said. "I have a letter from Heaven!" And he showed me a very old paper; it appeared to be a letter, starting with the words, "I, Jesus, write this letter; it will protect you against every danger." Then followed many words which I could not understand! The man told me "I tied this paper to a dog during a bombardment in Berlin and sent the dog into the street. The bombs were falling around him, and not one touched him."

"You have to make a choice between this letter and accepting Jesus. This letter is not from Him, but from the devil," I told him.

I looked around and called a girl with a counselor's badge on her dress. I explained the situation to her and said, "Stay with me: one must pray, while the other speaks to this man."

Immediately the girl went to him and quoted by heart the warning words of Deut. 18:10-13. She was a "Navigator" and had followed the Scripture Memorizing Course, and knew immediately how to handle the sword of the Spirit, the Word of God. I saw again how useful it is to know Scripture by heart, thus being prepared for the warfare with Satan! Wherever I go, I see how by this method Christians get practical Bible knowledge! It is used in the campaigns of many evangelists.

I had to leave for the next meeting, so I told the leader of the place about the situation, and advised, "Try to persuade that man to give you the letter for a week. During that time you must try to bring him to the Lord." He did this very thing. First he got in contact with the man, persuaded him to give him the letter, and then showed him the way of salvation. He then accepted the Lord, and wholeheartedly agreed that the letter should be destroyed.

Divination By Use of Charms

The devil can be a good healer of the body! If he can destroy a soul by healing a body, he is willing to give the temporary blessing of health!

Witchcraft is not only found in heathen lands! I was reading recently of a little girl in Germany who was constantly ill. Someone gave her a charm (amulet), a little box which she had to wear around her neck. Immediately she was healed. Her health was perfect after that, but there was darkness in her heart. She seldom smiled, and at the age of twelve tried to commit suicide. An evangelist was asked to help. He inquired whether perhaps she was wearing some amulet. It took some persuasion before she was willing to hand it over to him, and she said, "Never open it. The one who gave it to me said it would be very dangerous to do so." In spite of this warning, the evangelist opened the amulet and found a little paper, with these words on it, "I command you, Satan, to keep this body healthy, till you get the soul to hell!" They destroyed the amulet and the child was liberated, but instantly became very ill. Later she was healed by the laying on of hands in the name of Jesus.

Lack of Knowledge Can be Dangerous!

In Germany, a well-known evangelist had a dreadful experience. A lady came to him in great agony. The expression of her eyes was terrible. The minister had the discernment to see that she was demon-possessed, and in his longing to help her, he laid his hands on her for healing. At the moment when he touched her, he fell backwards on the

22

floor and was unconscious for a whole hour! After recovering, he found that the woman had drowned herself in the river!

When I asked him, "Did you not know that you may never touch a person who is demon-possessed?" he confessed that he had not known that it was dangerous.

Here was a man with a thorough theological training, much Bible knowledge, a heart full of love to help people, but he failed for lack of knowledge.

Jesus said, "Cast out demons . . . lay hands on the sick" (Mark 16:17, 18). He did not say: "Lay hands on the demon-possessed."

The Power of the Blood of Jesus

We should never deal with people who are under the direct influence of a demon, without claiming the protection or covering of the blood of Jesus! We overcome by the blood of the Lamb (Rev. 12:11). Though we don't understand this, we experience that God meant His promises if we, in obedience, act on the Word of God! The foolishness of God is so much wiser than the wisdom of the wise (1 Cor. 1 and 2). Only "faith-knowledge" can grasp these things!

We must also remember that the normal and safe position for every believer is "crucified with Christ" (Rom. 6:6).

If in the conflict with satanic powers the children of God claim the shelter of the blood upon the uncrucified flesh, they remain open to the workings of the spirits of evil.

Mrs. Penn-Lewis writes: "To speak of the blood cleansing the heart from sin and protecting, and not to understand as the correlative truth, the believer 'crucified together with Christ,' is failing to apprehend the full power of the work of redemption at Calvary."

Wisdom Needed

How much we need the discernment of the Holy Spirit, that we may discern the spirits and not be fooled! In Matt. 24:24 we read, concerning these last days, "For there shall arise false Christs, and false prophets, and shall show great signs and wonders, insomuch that, if it were possible, they shall deceive the very elect."

The enemy, when he appears as an angel of light, is more dangerous than when he rages as a roaring lion (2 Cor. 11:14)!

A pastor's wife once told me that there was darkness in her soul. She was a dear child of God, knowing that witchcraft sins are an abomination in the sight of God. But once, when she was ill, she consulted a doctor in order to find the right treatment. In her absence, he used radiesthesy over several drugs; he took a ring fastened to a hair and kept it swinging over a drug. When the ring went to and fro, it was to be the right drug, if the ring went round, it was not the right drug. I am not quite sure whether this was the procedure, or whether it worked vice versa. This really does not matter; but it is important that after the minister's wife used the drug thus selected, she came into darkness; so even this subtle use of witchcraft is a great sin.

But Jesus is victor! *He* liberated her from the darkness. The power of the precious blood and the use of the wonderful name of Jesus were stronger than the power of the enemy. The Christian life is often a battlefield! And the devil has about 6,000 years of experience in laying traps for the saints.

Jesus used the Word. There was nothing complicated about it! He just drew the sword of the Spirit and used it, then the devil left Him, first, for a season (Matt. 4), then fully, until the final scene on Calvary, when all the powers of hell were beaten (Col. 2:15).

The Power of Jesus' Name
(Excerpts from *Not Good if Detached*)

" . . . Christ, God's Son, holds [the true child of God] securely and the devil cannot get his hands on him" (1 John 5:18, Living NT).

How difficult it is to become used to speaking through interpreters! It is like trying to reach people "round the corner." As the listener's eyes are on the interpreter, the speaker is more or less out of touch with his audience. There is, however, one good thing about it—one has time for prayer while speaking!

Today I have an especially fine interpreter. He loves the Lord with all his heart, and it is pure delight to work together—such a contrast to indifferent interpreters! We are guests in the same home, and since we must speak again in the evening, there is time to chat together! Suddenly I ask, "Why is there so much darkness in you?"

"What do you mean?"

"There is no joy of the Lord in your eyes. In the parable of the vine and the branches, the Lord says, 'That my joy might remain in you, and that your joy might be full.' Where is that joy?"

"I don't know!"

"I think perhaps I know! May I speak? When you were converted from Shintoism to the Lord, you turned your back on the demons, but the demons have not turned their back on you!"

In surprise he answers, "That is true! But please don't tell the missionaries. They may think I have gone back to Shintoism."

"Demons are no 'ism'. They are realities as well as angels, and as you, and as I am! You lack a knowledge of the riches that are yours in Jesus! You need not remain in darkness any longer. In the name of Jesus and through the blood of the Lamb we have the victory. In His name you can drive out the demons and withstand Satan."

Together we read and obey the glorious promise and command in Mark 16:15-18, and then the Lord performs the miracle and completely liberates His child.

A few weeks later, we meet again. "Not only am I free," he says, "but my wife and my children also!" All hail the power of Jesus' name. His wonderful name is all powerful in heaven and on earth—that name above every name!

Many missionaries have given their all—money, family, and homeland—but they do not take all the riches offered to them in God's Word. Theologically their training has often been basic; but would not a study of God's Word teach them that to cast out demons and heal the sick would make them more fruitful, and should glorify Jesus?

How many dark powers there are in the world! Yet we have nothing to fear. The fear of demons is from the demons themselves. We overcome by the blood of the Lamb, and His blood protects us. And what joy it is that we have the authority of the name of Jesus!

Those who are with us are far more than those who are against us! At our side is our mighty High Priest and His legions of angels.

Boomerang

At a conference of Bible school students it was necessary to have somebody to interpret for me, and this was done by a girl who found it difficult to understand my English. When I used an illustration involving radar in ships, she became quite mixed up, as she had never heard of radar before! I tried to help her, and said:

"It doesn't matter, we will try something else. A captain of a ship stood on a bridge" but she never had heard of a bridge of a ship, and did not say a word! I told her, "Read James 1:5, 'If you want to know what God wants you to do, ask Him, and He will gladly tell you, for He is always ready to give a bountiful supply of wisdom to all who ask Him; He will not resent it.' You lack the wisdom to interpret for Corrie ten Boom, and this is the address where you can get it!"

But it was too late. She burst into tears. A Japanese who "loses face" is lost, you cannot do anything with him! I asked the leader of the conference if there was another interpreter, but he told me there was not! So here I was, with a message for the young people before me! Some of them had problems, and the answers could be found in the Bible that I had in my hand. For what reason was I unable to bring God's message to them? Here was the devil at work! The first step on the way to victory is to recognize the enemy. The devil is a conquered enemy, and we have the privilege and the authority to fight him in the name of Jesus! I turned to the girl and said:

"Dark power, that hinders that girl from interpreting God's message . . . I command you in the name of Jesus to leave her alone! She is meant to be a temple of the Holy Spirit, not your temple!"

As I spoke, the girl was set free! She was able to interpret fluently, and we had a meeting that was greatly blessed. So, what the devil had meant to be an illustration of his victory, became a boomerang and showed the power of Jesus Christ and His name.

No Advertisement

Years ago when Dr. Torrey Johnson from the U.S.A. came to Holland to start Youth for Christ work, there was much opposition, and in the newspapers appeared the dirtiest articles about him! Cartoons were printed and the meanest accusations against him were published! When Torrey Johnson arrived, there were no buildings large enough for his meetings. The best advertisement had been made by the enemy! We can learn from such an experience, and we must be careful not to advertise the devil by talking too much about him and his devices!

Some time ago I heard that in India there was a man who had all the symptoms and powers that the Antichrist or his helper will have in the last days! I decided to find out more details to be able to warn more people about him, but when I asked the Lord to guide me and help me to find out, He said, "Don't speak about the Antichrist, speak about Me!" I learned a great lesson! Although we must know and warn each other about the enemy, because lack of knowledge can mean danger, we must not give too much time and words to such warning. The Holy Spirit is on earth to glorify Jesus! We are the temple of the Holy Spirit, and so our task is to be used by Him as channels of streams of living water, for the glorification of Jesus.

"Go ye and teach all nations!" We have a story to tell to the nations, and that is the story of light and love! "We preach Christ . . . the power of God" (1 Cor. 1:23, 24).

Too Many Cakes and Pies

In South Africa, I received a telephone call, "Corrie, will you help us! There is a demon-possessed girl here and we don't know what to do!"

I was not happy. I have no special gift to cast out demons, nevertheless I believe that we must never refuse when God calls us! If we don't cast out demons, who must do it? Beelzebub perhaps? Why don't I like it? There is no real fear! Fear of demons is from the demons themselves. But it is always a terrible thing to see a demonstration of the powers of darkness in a human being. I called a friend who had a car, and told her the situation, but she answered, "You know, Corrie, I am always available with my car, but today I can't come! This whole day I must make pies for the church party tomorrow!"

I was angry and put down the receiver. The telephone was in a room where three pastors were visiting. I turned to them and said, "There are too many pies and too many demons in your churches!"

What did I mean? I have nothing against the pies and cakes in the church parties. The only danger for me is that, after some time of working in British countries, there is often "too much Corrie ten Boom," and I have to go on a diet! But how much time is wasted by making the finest and most delicious cakes and pies, when so many people have never heard the gospel! Jesus died for the sins of the whole world, but how many do not know that He died for them?

It can happen that in the house just next to the kitchen where many hours are spent to bake pies for the church live people who have a soul to save or be lost for eternity. "Let us redeem the time, the days are evil!"

There are too many demons in our churches! What do people do with a person who is obsessed or possessed? They go to a psychiatrist who gives shocks! That means solving a great problem in a small way, and that is always dangerous!

One of the pastors took me to the demon-possessed girl.

However, there was defeat that day! I never understood why! Was there perhaps anger or resentment in my heart? That could have been the reason! For if we give room to any sin, we ally ourselves with the enemy, and we stand powerless in the battle!

How We Need Guidance

In New Zealand, I told a group of ladies who came regularly together for prayer some of the experiences described in this booklet. One said, "Now I understand what is the matter with my neighbor's little girl! I fear that she is demon-possessed! Does distance exist for God, or can we cast out the demons from here?"

We all went on our knees, and in the name of Jesus commanded the demons in the little girl to leave her alone! When the lady came home, her neighbor came to her and told her, "My little girl is healed, she is quite normal." How they rejoiced! But an hour later, another neighbor came to her and said, "My little girl has the same disease as the neighbor's child!"

The lady understood that we had partly failed, because we had not forbidden the demons to go into anyone else! Together with other Christians they cast out the demons from the second child, and told them to go to hell, where they belong!

I am not quite sure whether we may do this last thing. A missionary in Africa told me that this must be said by the Lord Himself! In Jude we read that even the archangel Michael said to the devil: "The Lord rebuke thee" (Jude 9). But since I had that warning I have forbidden the demons in Jesus' Name to come back to the same person, or into anyone else, and told them to go to that place to which God commanded them to go. How we need wisdom! But in James 1:5 we read the joyful promise:

"If you want to know what God wants you to do, ask Him, and He will gladly tell you, for He is always ready to give a bountiful supply of wisdom to all who ask Him; He will not resent it " (Living NT).

. . . . .

"What can we ever say to such wonderful things as these? If God is on our side, who can ever be against us? Since He did not spare even His own Son for us but gave Him up for us all, won't He also surely give us everything else? . . . But despite all this, overwhelming victory is ours through Christ who loved us enough to die for us. For I am convinced that nothing can ever separate us from His love. Death can't, and life can't. The angels won't, and all the powers of hell itself cannot keep God's love away. Our fears for today, our worries about tomorrow, or where we are—high above the sky, or in the deepest ocean—nothing will ever be able to separate us from the love of God demonstrated by our Lord Jesus Christ when He died for us" (Rom. 8:31, 32, 37-39, Living NT).